PRICE: $19.95 (\$\$\$/IIC)

YES! EVEN MORE CANADIANS!

Hysterically Historical Rhymes

GORDON SNELL

With caricatures by
AISLIN

McArthur & Company
Toronto

FIRST PRINTING

Canadian Cataloguing in Publication Data

Snell, Gordon
Yes! even more Canadians!: hysterically historical rhymes

ISBN 1–55278–153–4

1. Celebrities – Canada – Poetry. 2. Humorous poetry, English.
3. Canadian wit and humor, Pictorial. I. Aislin. II. Title.

PR6069.N44Y47 2000   821'.914   C00–931320–6

Cover Illustration by *AISLIN*
Layout, Design and Electronic Imaging by *MARY HUGHSON*
Printed and Bound in Canada by
TRANSCONTINENTAL PRINTING

McArthur & Company

322 KING STREET WEST, SUITE 402, TORONTO,
ONTARIO, CANADA, M5V 1J2

The publisher would like to acknowledge the financial support of the
Government of Canada through the Book Publishing Industry Development
Program (BPIDP) for our publishing activities. The publisher further wishes to
acknowledge the financial support of the Ontario Arts Council for our publishing program.

YES! EVEN MORE CANADIANS!

Hysterically Historical Rhymes

Contents

THE LOON

(The Loon, featured on the Canadian dollar coin, is one of the world's oldest birds. It nests on lakes and rivers, and is known for its weird and distinctive calls)

Sing a song of sixpence
And never mind the tune.
We've got a dollar coin here
To celebrate the Loon.

Loons deserve your praises
Loons deserve your cheers
Loons have been around now
At least ten thousand years!

We can sound like wolves do
Howling in the night.
Even when we're laughing
It gives them all a fright.

Our portrait's on the coinage
Which ought to make us glad
But they're calling it the Loonie
Which really makes us mad!

PETER EASTON
(early 17th century)

(Peter Easton's swashbuckling energy and cheery personality made him one of the most colourful pirate leaders of his time. Choosing Newfoundland as his base, he plundered so many vessels that he made a fortune, escaping all pursuit with such success that he was called with some admiration "The Pirate Admiral")

*(These verses match the tune of the old sea-shanty,
"Bobby Shafto went to sea")*

Peter Easton went to sea
Sword and pistol on his knee
"I'm a Pirate King, that's me!"
　　Boasted Peter Easton.

He had ten ships fine and grand
Piracy was what he planned
When he came to Newfoundland
　　"Admiral" Peter Easton.

There at Harbour Grace he stayed
Up and down the coast he'd raid
"There's a fortune to be made!"
　　Gloated Peter Easton.

Fishermen to join him came
Drawn to him by loot and fame
Many of them took his name,
    Praising Peter Easton.

Scores of vessels he did seize,
English, French and Portuguese,
Plundering them all with ease,
    How they hated Easton!

To Cuper's Cove he made a trip
Took a merchant in his grip
Kept him weeks on board his ship
    Crafty Peter Easton.

Then he said: "I'll set you free
If you'll tell the powers-that-be:
'Send a pardon here to me,
    Here to Peter Easton.' "

Newfoundland admired him most –
Now he planned to be the toast
Of the Riviera Coast,
    Showy Peter Easton.

There he lived in wealth and fame
But Newfoundland to which he came
Still has many an Easton name -
    Praising Peter Easton.

John Graves Simcoe
Founder: Toronto

JOHN GRAVES SIMCOE
(1752 – 1806)

*(After a successful military career, John Graves Simcoe was
appointed the first Lieutenant Governor of the new province of
Upper Canada in 1791. His enthusiastic plans met with some
success and some disappointments, but they helped to found what
is now Ontario, where Simcoe Day is annually celebrated)*

All those who study Simcoe's story
Know he was very much a Tory.
He thought colonial solutions
Meant founding British institutions.
The land would flower with their insertion:
Democracy was pure subversion!

He named one river *Thames*, and he
Said there the capital should be.
He called it *London*, and would make
A road to link it to the Lake.

But people very soon would find
The Governor had changed his mind.
He said: "As capital, I aim
To grant instead *Toronto's* claim,
And henceforth *York* will be its name."

Said Joseph Brant, the Mohawk Chief:
"The Governor, in my belief,
All round our land has left his trace –
He's changed the name of every place!"

But Simcoe's main preoccupation
Was to enlarge the population.
Appeals for settlers were extensive;
The land they got was not expensive.

Whole townships too the Governor granted
To get the people firmly planted.
The eager methods that he used
Meant sometimes titles got confused.
He wheeled and dealed at such a rate
He could have thrived in Real Estate!

The many projects that he planned
To help enrich this vast new land
Were well-intentioned, great and grand –
But Britain didn't understand:
His masters didn't think it funny
If they were asked to send him money!

But using soldiers, he succeeded,
Built the roads the country needed,
And as was always his intention
Beat back U.S. intervention.

He started building Government House
Which definitely pleased his spouse:
His wife Elizabeth's pretensions
Were socially of huge dimensions,
And though the mansion was deferred
Elizabeth was not deterred.
Her High Society events
Were held instead in giant tents.

She played the Grande Dame with finesse
At balls where guests in sumptuous dress
Would gladly dance the night away
While stately orchestras would play.

When John Graves Simcoe had departed
His colony was truly started.
His name is in towns, lakes and streets,
And though he suffered some defeats
His zeal and eager dedication
Helped found the new Canadian nation.

SIR JOHN A. MACDONALD
(1815 – 1891)

*(John Macdonald began his career as a lawyer in Kingston,
Ontario, then entered politics, becoming the leader of the
Conservatives and in 1867 the first Prime Minister of the new
federal Canadian nation)*

John was, at twenty-one, a star –
The judges called him to the Bar.

Though soon, by some opponents' reckoning,
Bars of another kind were beckoning,
John thrived in party politics
And quickly mastered all the tricks.
Premier by 1856,
He saw that only Federation
Could forge a new Canadian nation.

So in Quebec the delegations
Began, some with persistent patience,
Others with fiery protestations,
To try to find a joint solution
And hammer out a constitution.

Eighteen days talking it would need
To get the document agreed.
So after many a deal, and dance,
Confederation got its chance.

It finally became a fact
When Britain opted to enact
The British North America Act.

Then politicians must debate
How to describe this latest state.
A Kingdom? Oh dear, no – because
A Kingdom's just what Britian was.

New Brunswick Premier Leonard Tilley
Believed such nit-picking was silly.
He said: "The Psalms, in my opinion,
Suggest we use the name *Dominion*,
For one of them declares that "He
Dominion shall have from sea to sea."

They all agreed upon the name;
John A. Macdonald then became
The first Prime Minister to stand
As leader of this great new land.

He did indeed think it should be
A land that stretched from sea to sea,

And so, to realize the dream
He backed a most audacious scheme
To build a grandiose creation;
A Railroad that would span the nation.

He thought that, as in all his deals,
Some patronage would oil the wheels.
Hugh Allen and his syndicate
Would think a railroad contract great
And Allen made most generous offers
To swell Macdonald's party coffers.

The syndicate would be selected
When John Macdonald was elected –
But there was something he neglected:
Surprise, surprise – he never thought
To tell the people he'd been bought!

But soon the Liberals told the world
And what a scandal then unfurled.
His reputation undermined,
Sir John reluctantly resigned.

But five years later, he was back –
The railroad plan was back on track.
This stunning engineering feat
In only four years was complete.

And soon it carried troops to quell
The second rising of Riel.
Macdonald chose a rash solution
And authorized his execution.
The anger and recrimination
Threatened once more to split the nation.

Somehow the Grand Old Man survived
And in the next election thrived.
He died, still in the driving seat,
His colourful career complete.
He had well earned his reputation
As Father of Confederation.

CAPTAIN JOSHUA SLOCUM
(1844 – 1909)

*(Joshua Slocum grew up in Nova Scotia and went to sea at sixteen,
becoming a superb sailor and navigator. After many voyages he
made history as the first yachtsman to sail round the world solo)*

He was an ancient mariner
From a century ago
And Joshua Slocum was his name
A name the world would know.

He was the first to take a ship
With billowing sails unfurled
And sail it on a perilous trip
Alone around the world.

On Nova Scotia's wildest shores
A wild young boy was he
And as he grew, he quickly knew
He'd run away to sea.

As cook and mate and skipper
Around the globe he'd roam

Then with a wife begin a life
Upon a floating home.

He sailed the seas to many a land
From Rio to Hong Kong
And everywhere that Joshua sailed
Virginia came along.

She bore him several children
Each on a different yacht
And as they floated on their boat
She cooked and sewed and taught.

There were lessons every morning
And when she got the chance
She'd play the grand piano
And even sing and dance.

For thirteen years of marriage
They lived the sailing life;
Then she died, and two years later
Joshua took a second wife.

She tried the floating housewife's role
But she'd rather stay at home.
So Joshua said: "Then all alone
Around the world I'll roam."

JOSHUA SLOCUM

JOSHUA SLOCUM'S BOAT

Diapers

In two years he had built a sloop
And it was called the *Spray*.
He stepped aboard in Boston
And he boldly sailed away.

Never had mariner before
Been seized with such a notion:
To face alone the great Unknown
Upon the restless ocean.

Through gales and fogs and storms he sailed
In lonely isolation.
He'd sing a tune, or with the Moon
He'd hold a conversation.

Harpooning turtles, shooting sharks,
He went his curious way,
And fried a dish of flying fish
Which landed on the *Spray*.

Atlantic waves, Pacific swells,
Like oxen he could yoke 'em.
No earthly force could stop the course
Of Captain Joshua Slocum!

He was at ease with V.I.P.'s
In each port he was at,
But in Cape Town, puzzled Kruger

Who thought the Earth was flat.

Once, lying ill with stomach cramps,
He said he saw appear
A ghost from the Columbus crew
Who took the helm to steer.

Not only storms were challenging
His navigator's arts.
A goat he'd taken on the boat
One day ate up the charts.

For nearly fifty thousand miles
And three years he did roam,
Then in his suit and black felt hat
He stepped ashore at home.

What seas he'd sailed, what sights he'd seen
From Sydney to Samoa.
His journey, many claimed, had been
The greatest trip since Noah!

Believe It or Not!

ANNA SWAN STOOD 7'6" IN HER BARE FEET WHILE HANK SNOW STOOD A BIT OVER 5'... BUT ONLY WHEN HE WORE LIFTS AND COWBOY BOOTS.

BOTH WERE FROM NOVA SCOTIA!

ANNA SWAN
(1846 – 1888)

*(Born and raised in Nova Scotia, Anna Swan found that her great
height brought her fame and fortune in exhibitions, tours and
circuses, as well as a husband of similar stature)*

Anna was born a normal size,
But gave her parents a surprise.
Of thirteen children, only she
Grew up so very speedily.
When she was five, though they stayed small,
Anna was nearly five feet tall.

Then P.T.Barnum – not a slow man
To seize his chances as a showman –
Saw Anna when she reached sixteen,
And said: "She'll wow the showbiz scene!
At seven feet six, and nothing less,
I'll call this stunning girl, I guess,
The Nova Scotia Giantess!
And she'll draw crowds to my Museum
Much bigger than the Coliseum."

Anna was not at all inhibited
By being so publicly exhibited.
Satin – one hundred yards or more –
Made up the costume that she wore.
Though people goggled at her height
She chatted to them with delight.

Besides her payment, which would be
A monthly thousand-dollar fee,
Barnum agreed that he would pay
A tutor for three hours a day;
And Anna learned to sing and play.

Anna was lucky to survive
A fire in 1865.
The building's windows were so small
That through them she could never crawl.
Museum workers smashed a wall
And rescued her, as flames did crackle
With pulley, rope, and block and tackle.

Travelling to Europe from the States
She met her husband, Martin Bates –
Shipboard romances can be lucky:
He was the Giant from Kentucky!
His height was seven feet three inches,
No problem when it came to clinches.

Married in London with euphoria,
They entertained for Queen Victoria.
Anna declared: "We will appear
On tour in Europe for a year.
The posters when we put them up'll
Announce:
    "WORLD'S LARGEST MARRIED COUPLE!"

They built on an Ohio farm
A house of most *enormous* charm:
Doors nine feet high no heads would catch,
And there was furniture to match.

A home for giants, His and Hers,
Just like a Dolls' House, in reverse –
A home to mark the huge success
Of Nova Scotia's Giantess!

LOUIS B. MAYER
(1885 – 1957)

(As a child, Louis B.Mayer came with his family to settle in Saint John, New Brunswick, where he grew up and worked in his father's scrap metal business. He moved to New England and prospered as a film distributor, then as a producer. He went on to found the MGM Studios and become one of the most powerful, feared and revered figures in Hollywood)

To New Brunswick – the port of Saint John –
Louis' people from Russia had gone.
Though scrap metal dealing
Was not too appealing
What deals he would do later on!

With film distribution he scored,
Then with Metro and Goldwyn on board,
He teamed up with *them*
To found M.G.M.
And the Lion in the cinemas roared!

He was Hollywood mogul and czar –
Film careers he could make or could mar.
Both Garbo and Gable

Were in Louis' stable
So were Hepburn, and Hedy Lamarr.

He changed writers' work without pity;
His retort when they raged could be witty:
"The Bible we call
The best book of all –
And who wrote that book? A Committee!"

His studio for years Mayer led;
At his funeral, enemies said
That of hundreds who came
Quite a few had one aim:
To make very sure he was dead!

GREY OWL
(1888 – 1938)

(Archibald Belaney grew up in the south of England, but went to Canada and adopted a false Indian identity as Grey Owl. He worked as a trapper and then became a conservationist, keeping his invented disguise throughout the lecture tours which made him a spectacular success in Canada, the USA and England)

Believing in your own publicity
Is quite a common eccentricity,
And Grey Owl fostered the belief
That he was practically a Chief.

He dyed his hair the deepest black
And with a hide thong tied it back.
He tried to walk the Indian way
And learned to speak in Ojibway.

He made sure nobody recalled
That his real name was Archibald,
Pretending that it wasn't true
That he was English through and through.

Brought up in Hastings as a child,
His ways were always somewhat wild.
He'd whoop and hoot, alarm the teachers
With snakes and mice and other creatures.
"I'll train for life outdoors," said he –
And slept all night up in a tree.

At eighteen, following his bent,
Away to Canada he went.
He learned to trap and to canoe,
And Indian skills and stories too.

And so began, bizarre and zany,
The life of Archibald Belaney.
In this most colourful of lives
He wooed and married several wives –
Not always bothering, what is more,
Divorcing from the wife before.

The one who gave him greatest joy
He met among the Iroquois.
Anahareo was her name;
She really shaped what he became.
She thought wild animals deserved
To be protected and preserved.

For conservation Archie opted –
Two baby beavers they adopted,

And soon a colony was planned.
The Parks Department thought it grand
And made a film whose stars so furry
Made audiences' eyes go blurry:
So cute and playful and endearing,
The Beaver Family had them cheering.

And soon with books and lectures too
Grey Owl's renown just grew and grew.
Through Canada, the USA
And England too he made his way
And there in London he was seen
Performing for the King and Queen.

As each rapt audience applauded
They didn't know they'd been defrauded,
And this fine Brave, so strong and wise,
Was simply Archie, in disguise.

But though he wasn't what he seemed
It was a worthy dream he dreamed:
A peaceful world where Man would be
To Nature, friend – not enemy.

At only fifty, Grey Owl died.
His hoaxes then he could not hide,
And those who'd praised him to the skies
Now scorned his masquerading lies.

So Grey Owl's pose as man of mystery
Was very soon consigned to history.

But now – the final accolade –
A *Grey Owl* movie has been made.
Pierce Brosnan, resting from James Bond,
The mantle of Grey Owl has donned –
Which must, wherever he may be,
Have Archie giving hoots of glee!

AIMEE SEMPLE McPHERSON
(1891 – 1944)

*(Aimee Semple McPherson – the two surnames came from her
first two husbands – grew up near Ingersoll, Ontario, and soon
discovered an oratorical flair that would make her name
and fortune as a barnstorming evangelist across North America
and in Europe and Australia too)*

The young Aimee Semple McPherson
Publicity-wise, was no dunce:
She grew famous, performing in person,
Some great evangelical stunts.

She would go to a crossroads and proudly
Proclaim that her work was the Lord's;
She would stand on a chair and pray loudly,
And the people came flocking in hordes.

Soon Aimee was driving them frantic,
Such a barnstorming style she could boast.
She wowed them beside the Atlantic
And across to the far western coast.

With marvellous Minnie, her mother,

To manage all matters financial,
One triumph led on to another
And her fortune grew very substantial.

Such worldly wealth pleased Aimee Semple
As she fervently preached the Good News:
She founded her very own Temple
Where five thousand could sit in the pews.

One day, Aimee suddenly vanished
From a beach not too far from her Church.
Thoughts of stunts then could hardly be banished,
Though thousands came flocking to search.

In a month she turned up, full of fury,
Crying: "Kidnappers captured me, folks!"
But lawyers before a Grand Jury
Accused her of staging a hoax.

The courts in the end didn't charge her
Though many still thought it a plot,
But her church congregation grew larger
And so did the money she got!

Her family relations grew bitter,
With many a law-suit and feud.
Her mother then claimed Aimee hit her,
And got lots of cash when she sued.

But Aimee's support just got stronger
And she stayed at the top of the tree –
And we wonder, if she had lived longer,
What a hit she'd have made, on TV.

WHAT HAS BEEN CANADA'S MOST IMPORTANT
EXPORT TO BRITAIN?

☐ Newsprint?
☐ Toilet Paper?
☐ ROY THOMSON?

ROY THOMSON
(1894 – 1976)

(Starting work at fourteen as a coal-yard clerk in Toronto, Roy Thomson became a radio salesman and then went on to control a world-wide media empire with hundreds of newspapers, magazines and radio and television stations. He also achieved his two most cherished ambitions: to be the propietor of the London Times, and a member of the House of Lords)

There was a barber's son called Roy
Who roamed Toronto's streets
And from his teens, his greatest joy
Was reading balance sheets.

He worked at selling radios
With flair and dedication
Till finally the chance arose
To buy a radio station.

Soon other stations came his way
And so did several papers.
More chances turned up every day
For Roy's commercial capers.

With love of wheeler-dealing
He was well and truly smitten;
Now he said: "I'll set them reeling
Way over there in Britain."

The Brits at first resented
This Canadian invasion
But the money he presented
Was a wonderful persuasion.

He soon became a social swell
With power and position
And even back at home as well
He got some recognition.

Toronto's Scottish Regiment
Said: "Be our Colonel." – "Yes!"
Cried Roy, "and my intent's
To wear full Scottish dress!"

One Scots employee made the crack:
"He has me near to tears –
As for the kilt, he's set it back
At least a hundred years!"

Roy said: "I never try to tame
My editorial pressmen."
Then Beaverbrook said: "I'm the same –

But then, I just hire Yes-Men!"

Oh, how Roy envied Beaverbrook!
And how he would determine
To be, like him, by hook or crook,
A Lord, with robes and ermine!

Not all Canadians would greet
With joy, Roy's royal rewards,
The day Lord Thomson took his seat
In Britain's House of Lords.

But now that Roy had scaled the heights
He longed for higher climbs:
Voraciously he set his sights
Upon the London *Times*.

The powers-that-be might fulminate
As Thomson schemed and stalked;
His Lordship only had to wait:
He knew that money talked.

They watched this brash Canadian guy
Do what he felt he must:
Grab major slices of the pie
And join the Upper Crust!

A third Canadian tycoon
Has said: "Now look at *me* –
I too will be a Lord quite soon,
And that will make it three!"

But Monsieur Chrétien saw his scheme –
"I veto it," said Jean.
"Let Conrad of his peerage dream –
The answer it is *Non!*"

"I'll sell my papers!" Conrad swore,
"You've barred my just rewards,
And now I'll never take the floor
In Britain's House of Lords."

So Conrad Black has been upstaged,
To Jean he had to bow.
But Roy himself would be enraged
To see what's happened now.

Today, he'd have to do without
Big Ben's melodious chimes –
Most of the Lords are booted out
And Murdoch owns *The Times*!

BILLY BISHOP
(1894 – 1956)

*(Born in Owen Sound, Ontario, Billy Bishop was an
unruly student who came into his own as an ace fighter pilot
during the First World War. He shot down a record 72 enemy
planes and won many medals, including the Victoria Cross.
His courage and his flamboyant personality made him a popular
celebrity, and he lived to play an important role with the
Royal Canadian Air Force in World War Two)*

No great delight young Billy found
In life at school in Owen Sound;
Nor did he seem to get much knowledge
At Kingston's Military College.

By discipline he was repelled –
In fact, he nearly got expelled.
But Billy said: "Before you bar me,
I'm going off to join the army!"

He went to England then to train.
Drilling one day, in mud and rain,
He saw above, a fighter plane.

High up it flew, alone and free;
Billy decided: "That's for *me*!
This army life is such a chore:
I'll join the Royal Flying Corps."

Many Canadians shared his aim:
As pilots, twenty thousand came.

Now Billy, zooming through the air,
Was brave and brash and debonair.
Down through the clouds his plane would swoop
Then nonchalantly loop the loop.
He chased his quarries with ferocity
Pursuing them at high velocity;
He'd dart and dive, machine-guns blazing –
His accuracy was amazing.

His style was just a bit ham-handed –
He damaged aircraft when he landed.
One general was a bit dismayed
When Billy, undercarriage splayed,
Crashed right in front of his parade.

One colleague said: "Though Billy's got
Great talent as a brilliant shot
An expert pilot he is not!"

But though he was inclined to crash
He had such daring and panache
His score of planes shot down was higher
Than any other Air Force flyer.
He once shot five down in one day –
And many medals came his way.

And somehow Billy did contrive
Through years of war, to stay alive.
Home as a hero then he came
To celebrations, cheers and fame.

The war was won, but Billy still
Craved the excitement and the thrill.
A company he put in place
With Billy Barker, fellow ace.

They said: "What Torontonians need
To start their weekends off with speed
Are aircraft fitted with pontoons
To land on lakes among the loons.
We'll save them hours and hours of driving
And soon our service will be thriving!"

But then they squandered any gains
By buying two old fighter planes
To use their flying skills at once
At fairs and shows, by doing stunts.

Sadly, the first big show to hire them
Immediately had to fire them:
The pilots, feeling blithely manic,
Dived at the grandstand, causing panic.

Then, though the thrills and spills were less,
In business sales, he had success.
In World War Two, his reputation
Enthused the Air Force of the nation.

His fame and talent were well suited
To get Canadians recruited,
And Billy Bishop would be partial
To recognition as Air Marshal.
No fitter honour could be found
To praise the boy from Owen Sound.

JOEY SMALLWOOD
(1900 – 1991)

*(Joey Smallwood rose from poverty to become one of the most
flamboyant personalities in Canadian politics, ruling
Newfoundland for nearly a quarter of a century. He finally talked
his beloved province into joining Canada in 1949, and thus became
the last official Father of Confederation)*

Some say it's weird, some say it's grand,
But all agree and understand
There's nowhere quite like Newfoundland.
The BBC in London knew it
And broadcast special programmes to it.

Subject of jokes, and admiration,
It thinks itself a separate nation
With its own music, style of speech
And even its own beverage, *Screech*.
Yes, Newfoundland has always known
It's like a kingdom of its own.

So Joey Smallwood, being no fool,
Decided like a King to rule

For there was nobody more showy
In all of Newfoundland, than Joey.

He said his family for sure
Came from the poorest of the poor –
So, well aware of what he'd missed,
He soon became a socialist.
His oratory, with passion fired,
Had all his audiences inspired.

And Joey's working life, meanwhile,
Was nothing if not versatile:
Newspapers, unions, radio –
At pig farms too he had a go.

And then he saw Canadian unity
As Newfoundland's great opportunity;
So he pursued his high intentions
Through referendums and conventions,
Becoming to his great elation
A Father of Confederation.

As Premier he won election
And people's loyalty and affection,
For his charisma meant they all would
Come out to vote for Joey Smallwood.
Joey his kingly mantle wore
With style, for twenty years and more.

He felt that now he had the chance
His people's fortunes to advance
(With help, of course, from federal grants).
The answer was, in Joey's eyes,
A programme to industrialise.

Although he wasn't one to shirk,
His projects didn't always work.
The fishermen who left the coast
Found town life hadn't much to boast.
Some unions now were shocked to know
That Joey Smallwood was their foe
As he pursued in ruthless fight
The policies he thought were right.

Opponents tried to do him down,
Called him a tyrant and a clown –
And yet his stature just grew bigger
And he became a father figure.
The jaunty style he had perfected
Kept getting Joey re-elected.

In the political arena
Canadians had never seen a
Champion who so boldy jousted –
Until, at last, the Champ was ousted!

Though later on he made a bid
To try to be the Comeback Kid,
He failed, which forced him to admit
An end must come, and this was it.

The politicans might uproot him
But idleness would never suit him,
And Joey didn't find it tedious
To write his huge Encyclopaedias.
Three published volumes of them stand
As lasting tribute, great and grand,
To Joey, King of Newfoundland.

GUY LOMBARDO
(1902 – 1977)

(Born in London, Ontario, Guy Lombardo and his brothers formed The Royal Canadians dance band, which became a huge popular success. Their regular New Year's Eve broadcasts became an institution throughout North America and beyond)

(If you are in festive mood, these verses can be sung – to the tune, naturally, of Robert Burns's "Auld Lang Syne"…)

"Should Auld Acquaintance be forgot" –
So sang the festive throng;
And *Auld Lang Syne*, as many thought,
Was Guy Lombardo's song.

On TV and on radio
It moved them all to tears
When played on Guy Lombardo's show
For nearly fifty years.

Guy's family was musical
And they could all be seen
At gigs in many a local hall
When Guy was just fifteen.

The Royal Canadians was the band
And with it Guy struck gold.
The records boomed in many a land –
One hundred million sold.

Some called his music "syrupy"
But Guy Lombardo swore:
"It is the sweetest there can be
This side of Heaven's door."

For sixty years this sound sublime
Was famed both near and far,
And somehow Guy still found the time
To be a speed-boat star.

So let us hope now Heaven swings
To Guy Lombardo's beat
And angels sweetly pluck the strings
While cherubs tap their feet.

>   For Auld Lang Syne, och aye,
>   For Auld Lang Syne –
>   Let's drink a New Year toast to Guy
>   For Auld Lang Syne!

THE DANGER of SPEAKING DOWN to PEOPLE · JKG

JOHN KENNETH GALBRAITH
(born 1908)

*(John Kenneth Galbraith was born at Iona Station, Ontario,
and educated at Ontario Agricultural College and then at
Berkeley and Cambridge University. One of the world's most
celebrated economists, he has spent much of his life teaching
at Harvard, has been an adviser to several US Presidents,
and written many influential books)*

The singular skills of John Kenneth
Have taken him right to the zenith
And there at the peak
With insights unique
What brilliant volumes he penneth!

In stature, John Kenneth Galbraith
Is certainly far from a wraith.
His brain-power and height
Made his rivals look slight –
No wonder his fans have such faith.

His views about things economic
Had an impact no less than atomic
Each treatise and book
Made all other views look
Like something you'd read in a comic!

"The olympics can no more have a deficit than a man can have a baby." Jean Drapeau

JEAN DRAPEAU
(1916 – 1999)

*(Jean Drapeau was Mayor of Montreal for nearly thirty years,
and dedicated himself to grand and sometimes costly plans
to give the city the style and high profile it still enjoys today)*

Jean Drapeau didn't care to frolic –
In fact, he was a workaholic.
By day and night he gave his all
For his beloved Montreal;
He even slept at City Hall.

Coming to power, he had the aim
To change the city's rakish name,
And many brothels soon were closed
And gambling licences opposed.
Pinball machines were even smashed,
And police corruption too he lashed.

But when the next election came
Opponents blackened Drapeau's name.
In posters now his rivals chose
To show him in a Hitler pose,
And thuggery, intimidation

And dubious vote manipulation
All helped to end Jean Drapeau's reign –
But phoenix-like, he rose again!

This time, to the people's cheers,
He stayed for nearly thirty years.
This most astute of city bosses
Towered like a neat, well-dressed Colossus
And cut a stylish mayoral figure;
Some mayors thought big, but he thought bigger!

A subway, malls deep underground,
Traffic solutions too he found;
Then Expo 67 came
To glorify Jean Drapeau's name.

He even thought there was a chance
To bring the Eiffel Tower from France…
The city did become the home
Of that huge Geodesic Dome,
And fairs and exhibitions all
Brought worldwide fame to Montreal.

But even bigger plans he had –
To host the next Olympiad;
And once the city had been chosen,
Building took off like an explosion –
And as construction grew and grew
The costs began exploding too.

Yet Drapeau's faith remained unsinkable –
A deficit was quite unthinkable.
Although the bills came thick and fast,
Olympic glory came at last.

There in the stadium stood the Mayor,
Now basking in the spotlight's glare.
He raised the flag into the air –
The cheering crowds threw up their *chapeaux*
To see Mayor Drapeau raise the *drapeau*!

Later would come recriminations
And budgetary examinations,
But Drapeau with his usual wit,
Said: "This is not a deficit –
I'd rather call it just 'a gap',
And so, why should I take the rap?"

Jean Drapeau for a decade more
With pride his mayoral mantle wore.
Though there were times he gave offence
To some provincial governments
The skilful way he'd wheel and deal
Kept his electoral appeal.

So Drapeau's reign went on and on
Like an Olympic marathon.
No wonder that his fans would call
Jean Drapeau *Mister Montreal*.

RENÉ LÉVESQUE
(1922 – 1987)

(René Lévesque was a celebrated broadcaster before he entered politics as a Liberal. He later founded the Parti Québécois which was victorious in two elections but just failed in 1980 to get a referendum majority in favour of an independent Quebec)

Though he was small, René Lévesque
Was walking tall throughout Quebec,
Becoming, after many a schism,
The Champion of Separatism.

When he was young, he'd no ambition
To be a party politician.
A war reporter he became –
Then Radio-Canada made his name:
His style and passion brought him fame.

That fame would help him, it was clear,
In a political career;
And so he won a Liberal seat
And joined the Cabinet elite.

At first he backed with resolution
Lesage's *Quiet Revolution*.
But soon Lévesque would change his tone
And start to strike out on his own,
Fiercely proclaiming to the crowd
A revolution much more loud.

The Parti Québécois was founded
And drums for independence sounded.
Supporters proudly would recall
The words of General de Gaulle:
"Vive le Québec Libre!" was his call
Delivered from the City Hall
When he arrived in Montreal.

It took some years before Lévesque
Was able to persuade Quebec
To opt, in 1976,
For René's brand of politics.

And oh, what rage and consternation
Was felt that day across the nation –
Or anyway, in Ottawa
Where René caused a brouhaha!
He told them, when he heard them yelp:
"A tranquilliser ought to help!"

(Yet there were always those out west

Who thought Quebec was such a pest
It wouldn't really drive them frantic
To see it sink in the Atlantic ...)

But René didn't do his worst:
He played it very cool at first,
And talked not of a separate nation,
But "Sovereignty-Association."
This helped his devious intent,
Since no one knew quite what it meant.

René announced, being worldly-wise,
That he'd maintain the federal ties
And promised that he wouldn't end 'em
Until he'd held a Referendum.

He managed to procrastinate
About the question, and the date;
When they were fixed, Quebec would see
Intense campaigns for *Non* and *Oui*.

Across the province, to and fro,
They watched the heavy hitters go,
Jean Chrétien and Pierre Trudeau,
Urging the case for voting No.

Although Quebeckers as a whole
Resented federal control,

Sixty per cent of voters stated
They'd no wish to be separated.

Yet when the P.Q. won again
Lévesque's power soon began to wane,
And resignations would conspire
To make him ready to retire.

And now, although Lévesque is gone,
The fights he fought still rumble on.

MAVIS GALLANT
(born 1922)

(Mavis Gallant began her writing career with the Montreal Standard, then moved to Paris in 1950 where she continues to write stories, novels and reviews. She had success in France and in the USA but it was some time before she got much recognition at home. Eventually it came, and she won the Governor-General's Award with her collection of Canadian stories, <u>Home Truths</u>.)

The critics agree that on balance
No style can quite match Mavis Gallant's.
She lays pompousness bare
With precision and flair
Which display her satirical talents.

She had a disturbed, restless youth,
And her father she saw as uncouth.
Her *Montreal Stories*
Show very few glories
But many a bitter *Home Truth*.

In the paper, she got a big chance
To take up a questioning stance:
"Are Canadians boring?"

"Do plays set them snoring?"
And "Is Marriage killed by Romance?"

She went off to Paris, and wondered
Could she write there, or had she just blundered?
But the stories that came
Made Mavis's name –
The *New Yorker* took over a hundred.

In her tales of expatriate life
The exiles and misfits were rife.
Each social scene too
Where hypocrisy grew
She probed with an eloquent knife.

At home she was largely ignored
But at last they began to applaud
And now Mavis Gallant
Has found that her talent
Is lauded both here and abroad!

GORDIE HOWE
(born 1928)

*(Gordie Howe grew up in Saskatchewan, a hockey fanatic
even as a child. His genius was soon spotted by the Detroit Red
Wings, for whom he played for 25 years. His career continued even
after that, and his name appeared constantly in the record books
and is enshrined in Hockey's Hall of Fame)*

The countless fans of Gordie Howe
All thought their hero was a wow.
His hockey prowess showed up soon
Where he grew up in Saskatoon.

There Gordie learned to skate, we're told,
When he was only four years old.
At home, he practised day and night
Shooting with left hand and with right,
And sometimes made his parents grouse
By knocking shingles off the house.

Then by a scout the boy was seen
When he was only just sixteen.
Off to the Red Wings' Camp he'd go
At Windsor in Ontario.

At eighteen, making his debut
His first game saw his first goal too;
The first of many – he would score
In his career, a thousand more.

Bull-necked and burly, Gordie struck
With his fierce stick, not just the puck.
The other players sometimes found
That he had felled them to the ground.

With deadly skill he swooped and scythed
While on the ice his rivals writhed,
And those trapped in the corner knew
The power of Gordie's elbows too.

His whole career was nearly through
When he was only twenty-two:
He skidded, slipped and cracked his head –
Brain damage almost left him dead.
The surgeons saved him – just one trace
Remained – a tic that jerked his face.
His callous team-mates seemed to think he
Would revel in the nickname *Blinky*!

Soon Gordie's wounds had healed so well
He galvanized the NHL.
Eighty-six points would clearly sock it
To Gordie's runner-up, The Rocket.

His progress after that was stunning
As Scoring Champion four times running.

With Stanley Cups and MVP's
Gordie would lead the field with ease.
This hero, speedy and adroit,
Spent twenty-five years with Detroit.
But his career was not complete:
He managed an amazing feat.

At forty-five, he ruled the roost on
World Hockey's Aero team in Houston,
And – what would really gild the dream –
Gordie's two sons were on the team!

New England and Hartford Whalers too
Brought hockey challenges anew.

No wonder Gordie Howe's great name
Stands out in Hockey's Hall of Fame,
For in that Hall he earned his residence
Through terms of seven U.S. Presidents!

NORVAL MORRISSEAU
(born 1932)

*(Norval Morrisseau grew up on the Sand Point Reserve
in Ontario. A self-taught artist, he painted the legends of his
Ojibwa heritage on birch-bark and paper. They were seen by
an art dealer who brought them to his gallery in Toronto
for an exhibition which made Morrisseau an instant success,
as well as a huge influence in the Canadian art world)*

First Nations were indeed the first
In art and culture to be versed
And long before the whites arrived
Their painting and their carving thrived.

The new arrivals sent those Nations
To go and live on reservations
And there, though poor and most deprived,
Their art and culture still survived.

The Europeans lived apart
And had their own ideas of Art
And so they never got acquainted
With what the native artists painted.

But then Jack Pollock got to know
The work of Norval Morrisseau
In far north-west Ontario.
On birch-bark and on paper too
In strong, bright images he drew
Ojibwa legends which he knew:

Tales of creation, death and birth,
And human struggles here on Earth –
world where spirits can reside
With human beings, side by side.

One thing made *his* work stand apart,
As Pollock saw, from other art
Which durably and firmly stood
Painted or carved in stone or wood:
These works of Norval Morrisseau
Could be removed and put on show.

And so in 1962
Toronto's art world got to view
A vision startling and new
That came from the Ojibwa Nation
And caused at once a big sensation.

Now overnight the painter came
From poverty to wealth and fame
And Morrisseau was quite surprised

To find himself so lionized.

He'd given Art a fresh dimension
That broke with custom and convention.
Now other Nations' artists too
Adapted Norval's style and view
And Morrisseau had been the start
Of one whole school called *Woodland Art* –
And now their culture could expect
New understanding and respect.

But Norval Morrisseau would find
Not everyone would be so kind:
At home he'd hear some elders say
Their myths should not be on display.

But Morrisseau went on meanwhile
To shape his individual style
And Expo 67 came
To give his work a world-wide fame.

He'd played his pioneering part
And caused at last the world of Art
To view with new appreciation
The culture of his ancient Nation.

GLENN GOULD
(1932 – 1982)

(Toronto-born Glenn Gould could play the piano when he was three, compose at five, and went to the Royal Conservatory of Music when he was ten. Making his debut at thirteen, he was soon a star of the concert stage, which he eventually gave up to devote all his time to recording. His playing style was as individual as his lifestyle, and his recordings particularly of Bach's keyboard works are admired throughout the world)

For months, while Glenn was in the womb,
His mother in the living-room
Would play the piano every day;
She thought this was the neatest way
To give the child a perfect start
In mastering the pianist's art.

It seems that she was right, for he
Was playing by the age of three.
This infant prodigy, before
He read words, learned to read a score.
Toronto's Royal Conservatory
Gave Glenn, at fourteen, a degree.

And soon Glenn Gould was all the rage,
A star on every concert stage.
The audiences he'd amaze,
Not least with his eccentric ways.

In rumpled clothes he'd sway about
His long wild hair all sticking out.
Conducting gestures too he made
And hummed the music as he played.

And when Glenn Gould began recording
The fans' response was most rewarding.
He'd sleep by day, record at night,
And edit tapes till they were right.
Each phrase was shaped, no note was missed –
Glenn Gould was a perfectionist.

Then suddenly at thirty-one
He shocked and startled everyone:
"I'll play no more on stage!" he said,
"The concert hall will soon be dead!"
Glenn would no longer be on show –
Out of the limelight he would go,
A hermit in his studio.

He did emerge, his tales to tell
In films, and radio shows as well,

Which were as quirky and bizarre
As Glenn's style as a piano star.

His clothes were quite eccentric too:
He'd dress for winter, all year through.
Milkshakes and custard were his diet;
At night his phone was never quiet:
His friends would listen with great patience
To hours of late-night conversations.

The eighty albums Glenn Gould made
Continue to be loved and played.
And yet one day he told a friend:
"I think my funeral at the end
Will not of course attract a throng."
Let's hope he knows now he was wrong:
His fans in hundreds came along.

And Glenn Gould's music found a place
In capsules sent to Outer Space.
So maybe, in a million years
Some alien, exotic ears
Will, on a planet far away
Hear Glenn performing Bach, and say:
"Those Earthlings sure knew how to play!"

LEONARD COHEN
(born 1934)

*(Leonard Cohen grew up in an affluent family in Montreal,
went to university at McGill and Columbia, and was
one of the group of radical writers who transformed the
Canadian poetry scene. He became a singer and songwriter and
since his first record appeared in 1968 has kept a large and loyal
following of enthusiastic fans in many countries)*

Leonard Cohen wrote some poetry
   when he was just a student
And his words they were not tame
   and his words they were not prudent
His classy Westmount background
   he would never let deter him
As an avant-garde protester
   he knew fans would much prefer him.

Soon Leonard started singing
   and he gathered quite a following
In his pool of melancholia
   they were happy to be wallowing

His sombre way of dressing
   couldn't make him look much starker
And his glasses they were dark
   and yet his songs were even darker

And they loved to travel with him
   for they knew that they would find
He had saddened everybody
   with his mind.

His lyrics could be baffling
   but he never wrote a platitude
Even when he sampled substances
   designed to change your attitude
He was seeking sacred pathways
   and he wondered where they ended
But no faith appealed to Leonard
   even half as much as Zen did.

His forlorn farewells to lovers
   had a hundred variations
Suzanne and Marianne
   just had to hear them out with patience
Though the tunes were somewhat similar
   and the lovers could be scornful

What made the fans delighted
   was that all of them were mournful

And they loved to travel with him
   for they knew that they would find
He had saddened everybody
   with his mind.

DONALD SUTHERLAND
(born 1935)

*(Donald Sutherland grew up in Bridgewater, Nova Scotia,
and went to the University of Toronto as an engineering student
before his acting talents led him to take up theatre. He moved from
stage to film, and a long and versatile career in over a hundred
movies which have made him an international star)*

Oh what a credit to his Motherland
Is movie actor Donald Sutherland!
His acting talent was precocious,
This famous son of Nova Scotia's.

Though earlier in his career
He studied as an engineer,
He found the theatre's allure
More dazzling, if much less secure.

He went to England, where he trained
And early stage experience gained;
And then he turned to film instead:
The Castle of the Living Dead
Was Gothic stuff, in horrors rich –
And in it, Donald played a witch.

After more horror movie thrills
He showed his comic acting skills:
The Dirty Dozen was a smash,
Then came his biggest breakthrough, *MASH*.
As Hawkeye, Sutherland became
A celebrated movie name.

He's acted since without a break:
Five films a year he'd sometimes make.
More than a hundred movies now
Have seen our Donald take a bow
And demonstrated his ability
And quite amazing versatility.

Robbers, detectives, firebugs, spies –
His roles were often a surprise.
The painter Gauguin he portrayed
And Jesus Christ he also played.

He says he is a great respecter
Of all the skills of the director.
"A movie actor's there," he's stated,
"To like to be manipulated."
To back his reverential claims
He gave his kids directors' names.

Donald in recent times has been
Back home upon the theatre scene.

When asked: "Does theatre cause you stress?"
He answered very firmly: "Yes!
Film acting's stressful in its way –
Sometimes you throw up every day!
On stage you're stressed when you appear –
It's just a different kind of fear.
But both have got as compensation
Their own immense exhilaration."

So Donald Sutherland continues
To flex his strong artistic sinews,
Enhancing with his gleaming radiance
The galaxy of star Canadians!

GILLES VILLENEUVE
(1950-1982)

*(Born in Quebec, Gilles Villeneuve was a champion snowmobile
racer before he took up motor-racing. His daredevil style on
the Formula Atlantic and Formula One circuits, as well as
his personal charm, made him a hugely popular figure in Canada
and abroad. He was killed in a collision at the age of 32,
but his name lives on in Montreal's Grand Prix Circuit and
in the motor-racing triumphs of his son Jacques)*

No racer was faster than Gilles
He had such magnetic appeal
    He first took the lead
    At phenomenal speed
When he raced in his sleek snowmobile
    VROOM, VROOM!

When he went into Formula Atlantic
His prowess was truly gigantic
    In one year, he'd first places
    In nine major races
And the fans' jubilation was frantic!
    VROOM, VROOM!

In flying, snowmobiling or driving
He was mostly the first one arriving
    The risks that he'd take
    Would make other men quake
For on danger he felt he was thriving!
    VROOM, VROOM!

And when to Ferrari he'd gone
His star in Grand Prix races shone
    His career was cut short
    In this perilous sport
But Villeneuve's name will live on -
    VROOM, VROOM!

BRET "HITMAN" HART
(born 1957)

*(Bret Hart grew up in Calgary in a family of wrestlers:
his father Stu ran the celebrated Stampede Circuit for many years.
He has won the World Heavyweight Championship title six times,
and was a key figure in the battles for control between
the two big wrestling federations, as well as appearing in
film documentaries and TV drama series.)*

The champion, Bret "Hitman" Hart,
Always looked like a star from the start.
With his hold, the *Sharpshooter*,
His rivals he'd neuter
And tear them all slowly apart.

Bret's father the wrestler would say:
"Our cellar's ideal for the fray."
He had his boys plungin'
Down into 'The Dungeon'
To practise for five hours a day.

When Bret as a pro was appearing
His boyish good looks were endearing;
Though his hair in the headlocks

Was like stringy dreadlocks
His charm had the fans up and cheering.

His athletic and muscular bulk
Could cause other wrestlers to sulk.
In his dashing pink tights
He won legions of fights
With guys like King Kong, Snake, and Hulk.

Every wrestler must have the appeal
Of a good "Babyface" or bad "Heel".
Though their falls, like a dance,
 Are all planned in advance,
The blood that they shed is for real!

Bret's wrestling career was to bring
Many fights, in and out of the ring –
But his fame it still grows
And all Calgary knows
That *their* local boy is the King!

WAYNE GRETZKY
(born 1961)

(When still in his teens, Wayne Gretzky began his spectacular career with the Edmonton Oilers, helping them to win four Stanley Cups in five years. He later joined the Los Angeles Kings and the St Louis Blues. He broke over sixty NHL records and went on to be honoured as the best hockey player of all time – "The Great One")

A jersey labelled 99
Was lifted up on high
To shouts and cheers and many tears
When Gretzky said goodbye.

The man they call The Great One –
A name he truly earned –
Always so proud to please the crowd,
To Edmonton returned.

For here his greatest triumphs
Those cheering crowds inspired.
It was a blow for them to know
That Gretzky had retired.

This skinny kid from Brantford
Fulfilled his boyhood dream
And made his name and gained his fame
Upon the Oilers' team.

The hockey records tumbled
The scores they mounted up.
The sparkling goals arrived in shoals
So did the Stanley Cup.

He scored more goals than anyone
In all the NHL.
He never missed with his assists –
Oh how those records fell!

The day that Wayne and Janet
Up to the altar went,
The grand parades and accolades
Were like a royal event.

Wayne Gretzky's sporting image
Was always squeaky clean,
So he got lots of TV spots
For products on the screen.

He also played for Canada
With passion and with pride:
The Maple Leaf in his belief

Adorned the greatest side.

And in the States, the President
Would even bow before him:
He was so famed that Reagan claimed
He'd swap all Texas for him!

"Just one more year!" the fans all cried,
"You're greatest of the Greats!"
Wayne said: "The Hall of Fame has all
My hockey sticks and skates!"

"So farewell to you, hockey fans,
For I must leave you now."
The rafters shook as Gretzky took
His last and final bow.

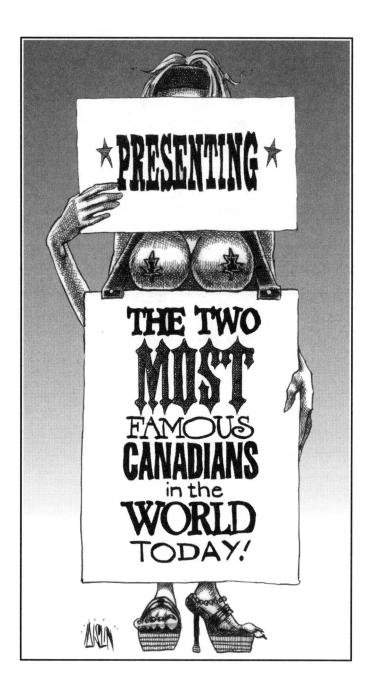

PAMELA ANDERSON
(born 1967)

(Born in Ladysmith, British Columbia, Pamela Anderson became celebrated as a buxom adornment of magazines and then as a star of the television series "Baywatch". Her career and her personal life seem to have been conducted in a constant spotlight of publicity)

In *Playboy* Pam was all the rage
As she came busting from the page;
In *Baywatch* no one could ignore her –
Once more she carried all before her.

Beaches seem central to her life,
For on one, she became a wife.
Clad only in a swimsuit, she
Married the rocker, Tommy Lee.

The pair did not exactly try
To stay out of the public eye:
After one amorous airplane trip
They claimed Mile-High Club membership,
And steamy scenes would somehow get
Exposed upon the Internet.

Pam had breast implants in, then out –
Events the papers wrote about,
Just as they told the sordid tale
Of Tommy ending up in jail
For beating Pamela – in due course
The marriage ended in divorce.

But later, saying that he went
To train in Anger Management
Tommy regretted his attack
And wanted Pam to take him back.
Where could this touching plea be seen –
Where else but on the TV screen?

It seems that Pamela was viewing:
Instead of crying: "Nothing doing!"
She liked this very public wooing
And planned to wed again, once more
On a Pacific Ocean shore.

They chose a beach in Malibu
To say again the words "I do."
This time they'd really have a ball
And wed with nothing on at all.

Could this be naked eccentricity
Or one more chance to get publicity?
It is a far cry, certainly,
From life in Ladysmith, B.C.

CELINE DION
(born 1968)

(Celine Dion grew up in Charlemagne, Quebec,
in a musical family, and composed her first song at the age
of twelve. She went on to become a world-famous singing star,
selling millions of records and winning Oscars for movie theme
songs, as well as a host of other awards.)

"My heart," declared Celine Dion,
"Will certainly go on and on,
And on and on and on and on,
Just like the endless song I sang
The night the ship's alarm bells rang
And everyone began to panic
Aboard the stately, doomed *Titanic*.
My voice of course remained to float
Upon the waves – unlike the boat."

This future star pop-music queen
Was born the youngest of fourteen.
At five, the tuneful tot would be
Performing with the family –
An infant prodigy was she.

When she was twelve, Celine Dion
Composed her very first *chanson*.
For René Angelil, the demo
Caused him to say: "Now, take a memo!
This little girl is going far –
I plan on making her a star.
And to be sure her records sell,
I'll be her manager as well."

So in her teens the young Celine
Was launched upon the music scene.
She very quickly reached the top
And then she never seemed to stop.

Most of the songs Celine recorded
With praise and prizes were rewarded.
Some envious glances she might get
From Shania Twain and Morrissette
But as for rivals, she could flatten 'em
With countless discs of gold and platinum.

Albums like *Falling into You*
Meant her success just grew and grew.
An Oscar came when she released
The theme for *Beauty and the Beast*.

Let's Talk About Love was one big title –
And to her, love was always vital.

It featured in most everything
Celine composed or chose to sing.

Some critics, looking for her faults,
Said she was wallowing in schmaltz;
One even dared compare her sound
To being in maple syrup drowned.

Love ruled her music, and her life,
For she became her guru's wife:
René she wed, once and for all,
At Notre Dame, in Montreal.

Not *once* and for all, as things turned out:
In case there should be any doubt,
Just five years later they'd decide
To act again as groom and bride.
A farewell concert she would do
(The latest one of quite a few)
Then to Las Vegas they were heading
To stage a most flamboyant wedding.

A ballroom was, for this event,
Transformed into a Bedouin tent.
Celine's dress looked like gold enamel
And dazzled every watching camel.

Jugglers performed, musicians played,

A belly-dancer writhed and swayed.
The pair on chairs were carried in
And then the wedding could begin.
They both held candles, then drank up
In turn, wine from a golden cup.

The ritual wasn't over yet:
They each put on a coronet,
And all this weird, elaborate show
Took up twelve pages in *"Hello!"*

Now some, bored by the goings-on
Of René and Celine Dion
Might only hope, with many a sigh,
This time, *"Hello!"* might mean: *"Goodbye!"*
Though others think that outlook's noir
And would prefer an *"Au Revoir!"*

YES! EVEN MORE CANADIANS!

AUTHOR'S NOTE

Encouraged by the popular success of our first two books, *Oh, Canadians!* and *Oh, No! More Canadians!*, Aislin and I have been delighted to parade this further line-up of celebrated Canadian figures past and present. As always, I have been immensely impressed by the variety and vitality of these Canadian characters, who have made their names in politics, piracy, painting, literature, music, showbusiness, sport, flying, motor-racing and round-the-world-sailing.

I would like to thank the Canadian Embassy in Dublin and the London Library for their great assistance in research, and my friends Michael Phillips and William Agar for their help and advice. I am also grateful to Marsha Boulton for her entertaining biographies in her splendid *Just a Minute* series of books.

My huge thanks and admiration go to Aislin, who has triumphed once again with a superb gallery of illustrations, and to our publisher Kim McArthur for her constant encouragement, insights and dynamic enthusiasm.

Gordon Snell

YES! EVEN MORE CANADIANS!

CARTOONIST'S NOTES

Let me add my thanks at this end to three individuals whose help was crucial in the production of this book:

Mary Hughson, for her always professional book design.

Pat Duggan of *The Montreal Gazette* library.

Gaëtan Côté, again of *The Gazette*, for quality control.

Aislin